THE PORTAGE POETRY SERIES

SERIES TITLES

Do Not Feed the Animal
Hikari Miya

The Watching Sky
Judy Brackett Crowe

Let It Be Told in a Single Breath
Russell Thorburn

The Blue Divide
Linda Nemec Foster

Lake, River, Mountain
Mark B. Hamilton

Talking Diamonds
Linda Nemec Foster

Poetic People Power
Tara Bracco (ed.)

The Green Vault Heist
David Salner

There is a Corner of Someplace Else
Camden Michael Jones

Everything Waits
Jonathan Graham

We Are Reckless
Christy Prahl

Always a Body
Molly Fuller

Bowed As If Laden With Snow
Megan Wildhood

Silent Letter
Gail Hanlon

New Wilderness
Jenifer DeBellis

Fulgurite
Catherine Kyle

The Body Is Burden and Delight
Sharon White

Bone Country
Linda Nemec Foster

Not Just the Fire
R.B. Simon

Monarch
Heather Bourbeau

The Walk to Cefalù
Lynne Viti

The Found Object Imagines a Life: New and Selected Poems
Mary Catherine Harper

Naming the Ghost
Emily Hockaday

Mourning
Dokubo Melford Goodhead

Messengers of the Gods: New and Selected Poems
Kathryn Gahl

After the 8-Ball
Colleen Alles

Careful Cartography
Devon Bohm

Broken On the Wheel
Barbara Costas-Biggs

Sparks and Disperses
Cathleen Cohen

Holding My Selves Together: New and Selected Poems
Margaret Rozga

Lost and Found Departments
Heather Dubrow

Marginal Notes
Alfonso Brezmes

The Almost-Children
Cassondra Windwalker

Meditations of a Beast
Kristine Ong Muslim

Torrential

"The *duende* does not appear if it sees no possibility of death," Federico García Lorca said of the mysterious power he recognized in certain poems, music, and art, describing them as if "baptized with dark water." The dark water of *duende* infuses Jayne Marek's remarkable fourth collection of poems *Torrential*. "What's Going to Kill You," she titles one poem, and other poems follow suit: boats, hot air balloons, forest fires, cancer and disease, the latter "swimming the long course / of our own body's fluids." In sometimes quiet, often dazzling language, these poems remind us of the fragility and beauty of our "brief ravenous lives" and of those whose fate we share and learn from: salmon, orcas, mudpuppies, the crocus, the "silent occult wings" of the owl.

—MELISSA KWASNY
author of *The Cloud Path, Pictograph,* and *The Nine Senses*

Jayne Marek's poems compel your attention with honed language that glints with intelligence and authority. Focusing on both the natural and the human worlds, these powerful lyrics recognize the competing forces of death and life, chance and design, the sublime and the profane. There are no easy answers here, but there is hard-earned wisdom, as in the message perceived in "the ancient face" of a salamander: "Grip the rocks and let the current bring / whatever feeds or harms you...." Read this book, it will feed you.

—ERIC NELSON
author of *Horse Not Zebra* and *Some Wonder*

Jayne Marek, in *Torrential*, carries us down a river of memories, lasting sense impressions, losses, loves, new meanings to past moments...and we begin to hear a deep chorus under her shining lines. These poems are a layered current of longing, tenderness, ache, and most of all, of unceasing surprise, the coursing shock, from birth to death, of being alive—as she puts it in her title poem, "the jagged lightning that spelled your name." This is a work of long travel, songs of the seaward torrent in which, wherever we each live, we're immersed.

—JED MYERS
author of *Learning to Hold* and *The Marriage of Space and Time*

Jayne Marek's *Torrential* excavates our tender mortality and the deep fear and care that cup it like a pair of mismatched hands. These poems are of the earth, full of blood and fire, fur and dirt. Here, language not only explores but complicates in distilled lyrics that pack a mighty punch. These are poems astonished to be in the body—and even more astonished to be outside it.

—KEETJE KUIPERS
editor of *Poetry Northwest*
author of *Lonely Women Make Good Lovers* and *All Its Charms*

TORRENTIAL

poems

Jayne Marek

CORNERSTONE PRESS
UNIVERSITY OF WISCONSIN-STEVENS POINT

Cornerstone Press, Stevens Point, Wisconsin 54481
Copyright © 2025 Joseph Marek
www.uwsp.edu/cornerstone

Printed in the United States of America by
Point Print and Design Studio, Stevens Point, Wisconsin

Library of Congress Control Number: 2025932495
ISBN: 978-1-960329-79-0

Cover art: "A Curtain of Rain" © Orville M. Running.
Used by permission of Philip Wharton.

Cornerstone Press titles are produced in courses and internships offered by the
Department of English at the University of Wisconsin–Stevens Point.

DIRECTOR & PUBLISHER
Dr. Ross K. Tangedal

EXECUTIVE EDITORS
Jeff Snowbarger, Freesia McKee

EDITORIAL DIRECTOR
Brett Hill

SENIOR EDITOR
Ellie Atkinson

PRESS STAFF
Eva Nielsen, Sophie McPherson, Ava Willett, Madison Schultz, Reilly Crous
Katie Schimke, Mai Kao Hang, Autumn Vine, Allison Lange, Gabrielle Sullivan

As ever, for Joe

ALSO BY JAYNE MAREK:

POETRY

Dusk-Voiced
The Tree Surgeon Dreams of Bowling
In and Out of Rough Water

CHAPBOOKS

Why Horses? Red Mare #13
River Triptych
Imposition of Form on the Natural World

COLLABORATIVE VOLUMES

Triple #10 (with Bethany Reid and George J. Farrah)

Company of Women: New and Selected Poems
(with Lylanne Musselman and Mary Sexson)

CRITICISM

Women Editing Modernism: "Little" Magazines and Literary History

A NOTE ON THE TEXT

Jayne Marek passed away unexpectedly in January 2025, having just completed final corrections to the present volume. *Torrential* has been published as Jayne wanted it, with the support and encouragement of her husband, Joseph Marek. Cornerstone Press is proud to offer up Jayne's final published work as a memorial to her talent, professionalism, and spirit.

CONTENTS

1.

Mudpuppy

In my twenties, before I knew who I was,
I climbed riverine wilderness, following the trail
across a stream whose shadowed trace hid
a sudden pulpy movement that halted me
in mid-step. It took a moment to discern
the speckled brown of a mudpuppy's body,
red gills like flowers wavering as it breathed
the air in the water, the water in air,
its ancient face that of a space creature
fallen to earth to bring a message:
Grip the rocks, and let the current bring
whatever feeds or harms you, however temporary
this water, this chance encounter, this
shade-lapped, early, humble reckoning.

What's Going to Kill You

How secretive it can be, swimming the long courses
of your body's fluids, nosing against veins and bowels.
Synapses light up as it passes. How you think about it

doesn't change its intention, whatever direction
it explores, beating past your eardrums, festering a little
in your alveoli. It's not urgent, it's slow to take,

like lily-pad goblets in the quotidian pond
of their lives. Think how their roots shift, down in mud
while leaves unroll at the surface, flatten out like hearts.

What's going to kill you never limits its reach.

The Swans

Something small to remember, from before the lesions:
gorgeous mown grass at Stratford, four American students
at the playwright's river where mute swans lingered
between sky and scour, the muck slow-shifting darkness,

as we unwrapped mutton sandwiches, and the swans
with their alien masks circled toward us, lurched
up the white-smeared bank toward Bruce, stabbed open
his lunch bag, and three of us laughed as they tore waxed paper
and scattered the food—*Piss and goddamn it, my lunch!*—
and Bruce on his feet now could not wave the monstrous birds

away from the one thing he had, this last year of his life.

Duende Verde

As if painting with fists and arms like Goya on the walls
of his studio at night, in fantastic wavering of lit oil,

the cantina singer wields her voice of flaming sand,
mouthfuls of liquor, bat wings spinning—

sound pours into Lorca's ear, the woman's musical
intoxication, and the poet himself is fog in the cleft

of a lightning-shattered tree, dreaming
that his hands scatter green ink across paper,

the stained oak table—
and the fierce woman whose hair falls forward
to her knees strikes the floor with black shoes:

Forewarned!

Unable Now to Atone

"Five men die in fiery balloon crash," UPI, 17 Aug. 1981

How heavily the balloon gondola hit the grass near him
ten seconds later meant that the survivor felt a shock
only in small degree secondary
to the violent strike of ground along his own length—after

the heart-open exhilaration when ropes dropped away
from the gondola, the riders whooping, sky
wider than he had ever seen. He looked up as wind stuttered

in the huge canopy with one stripe of orange
that was wrong, one snarl of fire not in the burner's
throat, blasting them higher, so that his animal self
burst awake and he turned away from his friends,
who stood still and stunned
as he jumped out—

he heard the balloon burning, the other men shouting
as the gondola sped upwards for a few more instants
freed of his weight—

Fire-Nerves

Summer smoke wanders from room to room,
scatters shreds of orange paper.
I am losing the words

for weather, the heights of clouds,
how broken they seem, how instead smoke's
never satiated. Now I see

fear comes from burning.
I want to tell someone

but the phone rings to nothing.
This was my safe place, I tell silent finches
who line the funeral fences.

These molecules were the owl.
This layer on a railing, two fawns
and their mother, or the mother

of someone. Ash as tremulous
as the touch of aged hands,

disbelieving: my old auntie,
aged eighty-nine, who ran
into the outhouse on the farmstead
and shut herself in.

Beautiful Graves

Down to southern Kentucky, taking my time.
The roads transform under my car wheels

to asphalt paths that barely crest the hills
and leap of their own accord, side to side,

skim the verge of overgrown bushes so close
I feel I'm threading past a herd of bulls.

The green pulls back when I round a turn
to find a bald hill with headstones aslant.

I stop, step into sun and humidity, push my gaze
into the weeds, see faint names in granite

traced by a scrim of dirt. Within a minute
a car pulls up with a sagging man inside.

His hard blue eyes, like my grandfather's,
scrape up and down my form; I recognize the set

of that jaw. I offer I've come to see
a great-aunt in the next town. When I name her

he says he's a relative, gets out, and we shake hands.
Seems he believes me—I don't look like someone

here to steal the headstones. He doesn't say as much.
Under his stare I agree to visit the old farmhouse

for half an hour, and we drive over; I compliment
the fresh paint on kitchen beadboard, duck my head

in the stairway up to the unused rooms. An old window's
sagging glass reveals a shabby outhouse

back of the lot. Neither of us gets past small talk,
so I repeat the aunt's name, and this grandpa's-cousin

stands in the yard as I drive away. I pass
more than one squashed turtle on the road

to my destination, rich red recent blood
congealing over the dark mess of the dead.

Understory

A dead dog, dumped in the woods,
presses into late-spring violets,
its hide caved between hips and ribs,
shoulder-bones like blackberry canes.
        So my husband tells me.

I stand on a path out of sight
of the carcass, looking up
into kindly green light,
a mausoleum of cedars,
        communal privacy.

I could step over to look
at the dog's face, sunken and mudded,
its eyes unable to respond
whether or not they're open.
        My husband doesn't say.

He knows I'd want to stroke the stiff fur,
strung as I am always
on my own wires. The poor flattened dead
unmoving, my hand open
        where no whistle hangs in the air.

The Boy in the Well

*"A 5-year-old boy dies after he was trapped
in a well for 4 days," NPR, 5 Feb. 2022*

Now the dead boy signifies there is no
grammar of hope anymore, the map's split
open one hundred feet deep to where the slow
dark film unreeled for the child. Heavy,
the rescuers dug down to their own great
alienation—so deep, they knew they were
ships sinking, shifting in gravel that whispered
like lessening breaths, to learn at the end
that, no, never again would the father
hold up a kite to show the boy whose eyes
loved Moroccan sky, blue as his own veins.
Now the sun fire eats the village of grief.
Now the mother wants only to retrace
her steps to the morning four days past,
the father cannot bear to look at his land,
his heritage that swallowed the boy. The
parents are breaking, the cows and donkeys
agog, even the curious slinking jackals
sense the void that answers the parents
who call and call, without words, his name.

The Cows

I drank the silence of God
Out of the stream in the trees.

—Georg Trakl

A thresher churns the filmy fields, out of sight.
So the cows tell each other, their wooly heads close
as they mourn how plastic wrappers snag the creek's path,
paper swaths sip in their cistern.
Everything is cold these days, murmurs the bell cow,
my heifer nowhere to be found.

She places her nose against barbed wire
until it almost pierces skin, and holds it there
while three pairs of headlights swim past in the gloom.
She knows this is not the only road, but it's one
the cows can see. The thresher whines down to silence.
A distant voice says *November* out loud.

Infection: Tether and Needle

this is what my blood looks like—

rim of a well seeping rust
a lost scarf snarled in mud
geranium petals blown from their stems

chokeberries crushed by the beaks
of ravenous sparrows

a penny lost in the street for a year
degraded to the color of neglect

under a streak of dawn, a cloud's arm
creeps toward a heart

*

strands of tubing pinned
to my arm as still as a pew

the soft throb of a pump telling its prayers

I have lived among these sounds so long
they breathe for me
in endless supplication for more time

*

beyond curtains, the sea reaches
its torn blind way along cliff rubble

harried by rocks it dislodges in the tide
that silently fills until it has to turn

withdrawing—
the same place ever changing

sea bed stalled in drift
that can unexpectedly
carry this water past the vanishing point

*

half-sounds and half-light
half-living, half-not

the IV pumps peep
solicitous as guardian angels
not sure what to do

as meds whisper through my limbs
searching for the hidden spider
that crouches under my small knuckle

that watches the blood-borne searchers pass
one pulse at a time

*

here I am anchored lightly
by a meager tether and needle

the sheet, like fragile paper,
folds and wrinkles its cryptic messages,

outdoors, clouds roll on salt water
following the wind—

I imagine an otter bobs and sinks
in the pattern of waves near shore

surface spins where the otter dives
an oracle present in absence—

will my sheets be washed as if in surf
when I am gone

the bed, the shore new-made
erasing whoever had been there

Last Crocus

From the earth, I looked up into grasses
narrow and more beautiful than clouds.

They lifted with me, parted for me.
Their green brushed over and past

and I began to forget their touch
when cold wind stretched my sleeves.

Nevertheless, the air too was lovely
as autumn spun its orange blades.

I learned to desire more color
as colors faded: yellow mud clods,

the black bruise of a late beetle,
angular, stumbling toward lurid purple,

a skin of ice. A kind of drink.
I had waited so long to be—

offered my thin golden word,
opened my mauve gloves.

Ritual for Beasts

In spring, skunk cabbages unfold in ravines,
   spread yellow leaves and redolence distilled from salmon
who died here last autumn. Rain pressed their bodies deep.

Salmon return to open themselves completely. Home,
   where one must eat. Where creatures would choose to die

and where I too want to vanish
   into ten thousand welcoming touches
of soil. Not afraid to be consumed in my turn.

2.

Wolf Moon

How quickly it transits,
an arc of ice tightening
from west to east.

A rock
thrown into black water
shivers into the deep, empty belly,

carrying light down with it.
The full moon
steps from overcast into the cold

of January. Her feet trail
a dingy rag, the shadow
of Earth. One planet

tastes the attraction of another.
Winter is a cascade
of hungers,

wolves at the edge
of the woods, slipping like a tongue
between ribs.

October Salmon

1

yellow alder leaves on submerged branches
        waver
                like the fungal patches

                        on the skin of chum salmon fighting
          upstream in autumn

the slant sun
        coining reflections

2

            a fish
                like a seed
            must work up energy
        to burst toward its next existence

and the creek
        is a narrow byway of propagation and death

            plundering
                the collisions of water and bodies

in its natural speech

3

bright slash of daylight
          opens the bare tree arms

berry canes catch each other
        on the path
                with its steep drop

moss hangs but never falls

      following the rush and music of water-travel
        making its own snags

4

      broken sticks   feathers   bones
  stones   scraps of birchbark
flare in these rapids

         distorted
      by shifting sun
  lenses

runoff from mountains
  the fish will never

     reach
       yet they reach

5

     at the ends of their lives
       returning
   to the stream of life

salmon flex and thrust
  against one another
     amid the current and fallen logs

      in the imperative to spawn
and then die
  into their next existence

6

　　　　　here under the forest canopy
　　　　　　　　the water

so shallow one can step in
　　　　　　　and resist
　　　　　the pull at one's ankles

　　　　　　　one can imagine
　　　　　wading against the current

that shakes the fishes'
　　　　　backbones and ribs

　　　　　　　now bare

that shifts them as if
　　　　　the water itself

　　　　　　　takes over life

7

who was the first person
　　　　　to find this understory
　　　　　　　to learn

　　　　this pathway toward change

　　　　　these fish bodies subsiding

　　　　like pieces of cedar bark softened by the flow

along shore where ferns
　　　　　unfurl one question at a time

　　　　　　through thin ribs

8

a chum corpse rolls against a log
    a sad wave, a signal

to empty all of one's body
        into struggle means to accept

    it will strip our frames

Not an Urge to Die, Exactly

The urge to skydive, rappel, white-water kayak
is the urge to release, the urge to die.

—*Arthur Sze*

I remember the buck and roll of my body
against gravity—compressions of air, earth, water.

Rapids in the Snake River elbowed me
against rocks. A step backward

off a ledge in Yosemite let the clouds lean
across my lungs. Hard wind

battered my face as I clung like a cub
to the Piper's strut at seven thousand feet,

let loose. The tattered clothing of the world
tilted and slid awry.

Blind in the current's tumult; half-seeing the shoulder
of a cliff; seeing more than everything

how bones fracture with a private sound.

Orcas, a Prelude

We want to tell our stories without losing the truth of waters,
which live and change as we do over so many years
that we have the same grandmother.

Our language moves as currents between what is cold and colder,
a language about the bodies of fish, narwhal, sea lion, seal—
sustained by some of these, not others,

which the visiting gods eat. Now our families are fewer,
as hunger demands our shapes move
with wasting muscles,

we become narrower, shadows, parentheses, parabolas
that mark the sea wherever we travel. We kill;
we are killed; pain is the truth of waters.

The Point That Divides the Sea

In memory of drowned refugees

At the lighthouse's foot, someone built a breakwater
    of flotsam: single sandals, loafers of all sizes, half
        a gumboot, arranged by color—first, the indigos and teals
            of plastic slabs, one child's size with a Big Bird face
next to three adults' blues, a navy Topsider, then a green one,
    well-worn and sad, soaking into sand. One red
        Converse, squashed flat, twinkled with specks as sunset
          washed the Aegean beach, darkening the pink

flank of an espadrille, cuddled alongside an orange
    flip-flop with its left strap dangling. A few shoes
        in yellow, others grimy, barely white, and finally
the darkened debris of a wingtip and some torn-off
    soles, one with a hole right through, where someone's foot
        pressed hard on its journey to improper unburial.

Residual

a short trail of paw prints

across the snow
that covers the creek

wanders for a few yards

stops
in the middle

where the water

under fresh flakes
where the water

froze over again

Solo Dance

Lake Easton State Park

1

Alone, I leave my car
under parking-lot trees,
walk the aisle between bushes.
It's mystery, as late light
drips from an alder twig
while crowds of leaves shimmer
as if a performance's last notes
were spinning echoes
into the balconies
of velvet forest.

2

Woods open to a lake
with the swimming area stitched
by a string of buoys. Sky
reflects in minuscule puckers,
the meniscus boots
of water striders. They skate
in random fits
then speed away. A handful
of shadows scatter coins
across the shallow bottom:
Bravo!

3

Along the edge of the lake,
prints four inches across,
an inch deep in sand.
Like blossoms, petals evenly spaced,
four shaping each circle. Rounds

within rounds. A solo dance,
the houselights of afternoon still on.
I stretch out my stride
to match the cougar's,
my shoes three feet apart.

If One Can Speak Seriously of the Sublime

Salmon travel the long ways, tails bent against gravity, noses hooked by shadow. Living trees vanish overhead into canopy and take salmon with them. Salmon climb into sky; they swim behind and through the trees and earth. They swim in fog; they are fog that passes into an open stump. Wood tastes tassels of the sea, miles away. Scales glitter on rough bark in the rain forest. Sea and fog are rain, are salmon.

It is hard to die. Salmon come to death through hunger for home that drives them through seas, up a creek, scraping their yellow skins. The harps of their bodies loll in the songs of creeks lost in woodland. Maple leaves spin down. All would be hungry but for this hunger of the salmon. Hunger of bears, of foxes, of crows, opossums, wood rats, voles, the beetles, flies, ants, the roots of fir and cedar, the diminishing creatures with their own hungers.

A hollow tree is a mouth that has already said what it knows.

Listening for Otters

At evening, the neighbor knocks: *Come out*
and listen at the edge
of the ravine, she whispers,
for the baby otters playing. The water
unseen below us makes its own talk.

The darkness is a jacket
we hunch into, the day's fears
invisible now: the ambulance at her door.
Worry lifts leaf by leaf as we stand
in the chill. Tonight

will bring a full moon, but not yet,
and the clouds may thicken. Night calls of birds.
Things move on whether we're here or not.
Owl claws that scratched my roof yesterday
will not return. I don't know how

I know not to expect much,
just a rustle in salal bushes downslope.
He's all right now, she says on half a breath.
Nothing came of it. She can't see me nod,
our heads bowed.

We share the quiet,
attend to its depths, the cool
shuddering touch
of night insects beginning their work,
their brief ravenous lives.

Nourished

the form of a human body takes shape against a curtain

in half-light   an outline of limbs   a bole of flesh
and muscles   clay in a forever process of becoming

built to move up from rest   from need
from what has become of meals   of days that tapered

into sleep   what calculates hatred of this body so perfect
its weight itself a possibility   an enactment

a completion of foods   their mystery   thousands of flavors
their aromas   the necessity   of sustenance

why judge sustaining comfort of fat

it teaches any body about itself   its privacy
out of which it unfurled   and into which it will die

another iteration   a perfection   do not hate it

the body a balancer   of mind   all
in orbit around what is temporarily   the heart

Great Camas

Camassia leichtlinii

Green spikes today in the back yard—
as if a single night gave enough nurture
for the camas, come in their own time,
with private stars gripped in their fingers.

Be knuckled blue, you, signal the bees,
bloom forever. Let us, shimmering
multitudes of lovers, coax out your poetry,
stay through the dark, cling to you upside down.

Instar

Given that evening yellow blends with the shore.
Given bighead sedge that rusts along its spines.
Given the soft bellow of an unseen freighter.
Given that we climb through a fence.
Given the eye of an eagle that drops like an axe.
Given the bright bones of a porpoise corpse.
Given that we sink with every step.
Given two sundogs adorned by illusions.
Given that memory rides along our hat brims
and one tree moans, bent against another.
Given thistles, sand verbena, lomatium, fescue.
Given the humble.
Given flights of green dust.
Given that we are on our knees.
Given that darkness presses a far island like a fallen skyscraper.
Given lines of broken shells that lead into the current.
Given what takes us away.

Desert Devotions

for Francine

At evening, you could walk into the desert with your son,
a grown man, who in the horizon's halo seems both tall
and fragile, as if he were still seven years old,

whose voice loves the scorpions that come
out of hiding in the comfort of starlight, tells the lives
of families of burrowing owls, sand sifting

from their wings. The mineral scents of this valley
make a tea of air. It's hard living in desert
extremes, devotion and fear, as the creatures here know.

What has happened to them in the past
years of dry air and thirst drew on the strength
that shapes their spirits like cactus shadows

on pale dirt. You could keep going forever toward
the horizon in any direction. Talk has disappeared
into the tent of desert night. You will both be fed
and sheltered in your going.

3.

Torrential

Why not admit you expect the power
of a flash flood that pours toward you
out of the literal blue, a desert day
as you hike along creek beds? The water's
arrival like an annunciation
not of salvation but imminent
inundation? Think of wet fists
pummeling your ankles and calves
as you look down, surprised
by how fast it's coming,
at your knees already, this water
heated by the sand's frying pan
as rivulets find each other, swim together
toward your feet. You can't outrun
the water that froths up
at the base of saguaros, spatters
gray droplets across leather
cactus skin and hooked thorns
as you catch a last glimpse
of sky. You close your eyes
at the sting of minerals, the dirt
shoved up your nose. You think
that at last your unmoored feet
will carry you somewhere that answers
this moment: the hammer of water
a reminder of when you did not see
your mother's saucepot in hand swinging
toward your head that day in your youth
for something that you wouldn't
take back, and won't even now, despite
the evidence of a distant thunderstorm
up in the hills that you'd ignored,
the jagged lightning that spelled your name.

Not Interested in Jesus

Black goo on my knees and legs—I know I'm in trouble.
Mom said, *Go play in the yard! Don't come in so dirty!*
But I like to crawl under the tent of the big pine, amid branches
that droop across daylight. It's as dim as the library, where I sit
in a corner and pinch edges off pages to put in my mouth.
I am hiding beneath the tree. I have buried one of my small toys
in dirt. A naked baby doll, arms outstretched like Jesus.
I covered it up. I'm not interested in Jesus. I think about
the sweep-up, sweep-down of robin talk when the birds
stop flying at dusk. It's like evening light under the tree
this afternoon. I'm filthy, sap and needles stuck to my arms
and chin. *How did that happen?* she'll ask in her mean voice.
I'll look up, not quite at her face, as if it's a slice of the sun.

Stairwell

I dreamt into possible flight
at the age of four, a daughter hung in darkness
of morning, flickering, my mother
below in the kitchen. As a child I loved
solitude, not-being, undefined
by chopping and deseeding, the version of me
that my mother prepared with her back turned.
I had lied. As if any answer would suffice.
Her countenance was dark as apple flesh
in a wooden bowl, alive with juice.
                                      I thought
the silent stairs below me a parade of friends
framing a white space of anger.
A vision of falling wanted the child me
to accept its answer.

Going On

My father the child sits in the street banging glass out of manhole covers because he likes the sound and because his father, the laborer, has a heavy fist; it lifts and falls, lifts and falls. *My mother the child watches her father's hand rise and drop on her mother, and my grandmother is unable to heal her children who inherit the blows.* Rows of rough-shouldered apartments on Noble Street, Chicago's north side. *Shabby partitions in houses on Pleasant Street in Freeport, near where the rail lines cross, some heading south to New Orleans, some toward Chicago.* Trains hammer slowly past the Merchandise Mart across Clybourne's fractured concrete, *or on bridges above the Mississippi with its lazy brown murderous heart, its swells of drowned cattle and overturned tractors.* What keeps beating inside people from long-ago lives, what is around me, in my hands, in broken glass on asphalt, *in weeds sagging with soot along the endless drag south or north, rail lines that never end.* The Loop. Whatever is moving stops only for a time and then goes on.

When My Mother Says *Rattlesnake*

I envision my grandfather's face, a crooked stick
amid weeds. Between the farmhouse and the outhouse,
I walk into a clot of smells. A row of spots shifts
in half-shadow. I'm a kid, afraid, visiting Kentucky,
the old family property, full of heat and hunger,
animals crushed along gravel roads. Uncle Luther
was driving that pickup way too fast
as if he needed to tell everybody something
from beyond the grave where he ended up. Now
there's a black blur waving under the porch
and a broken plant pot seems to tilt toward me
as I leave that outhouse where I couldn't even pee,
it was so weird. Who'd look through those knotholes?
How does anyone stand the stink?
Back to the house, Grandpa spits and says,
Just a damn skunk and don't step over there,
ain't you learn to be careful when you visit?

Mistaken

Youths' ego and blindness, not exclusive to youth,
collapse from the weight of snow and take down
both the roof and whoever's on the ladder, trying to clear
drifts of words that showered down for days
or weeks, in a climate anyone should have known
would bring too much accumulation to handle.

Inexperience blurs your awareness
of what should have been the right place to settle,
the home you'd always looked for—as if
there would never be an accumulation of errors
in judgment, of any of your faults, qualities unequal
to this year's weather. Some ruptures can't be fixed.

Not So Much

a young friend of my brother's whose parents died early
inherited enough money to blow two years being stoned
and listening to hard rock on a new stereo system with speakers
that shook the university dorm room among his few friends
the pot heads' feet on chairs and music was something to talk about
all the time instead of about his mother's dark-rimmed eyes
his father's shoulders sloped like overused cushions the son barely
went to class for the two years it took to flunk out
at that regional campus his parents had never been able to attend
but instead worked their little mom-and-pop shop all those years
of long hours and yellow light as if seen through smoke
that never seemed to clear away to reveal a different life
I suppose they had yelled at the son to get up and do something
and knocked on the son's closed door the radio so loud
that words seemed as meaningless as the hours of work
gone now—like the parents and their money and even the friends
some of whom died early too what the hell happened

High School Dog Days

August rolls across the pavement, blazing
to the touch, like the long fenders of my
brother's old Chevrolet, polished to a high
gloss and black as a pool of tar. A vision,

an untouchable shimmer, the coupe
crackles to a halt in our ragged lane.
The guys in the back seat have to climb
over the half-mast convertible top—

stuck in a useless grimace, canvas torn—
wincing, cursing, yanking up their hands,
but by God it's the car he wanted. My
brother waits until his buddies are out,
elbows the driver's-side door and exits,
slack-hipped, knowing everybody's watching.

35-Cent Gas

Body of the Volkswagen my body, a folly.
Nights spent driving back streets, as if that would help me.
Summers when insects spattered across the windshield
in peculiar plenty. Winters when black ice jerked
under the wheels, flared my headlights along ditches. My palm
on the steering wheel balanced a joint, its bright tip
an extension of consciousness, a red satellite
that swooped toward my face then back past the edge
of the real. Kept me rolling, kept me on the road
driving, a damn teenager who didn't think ahead
and just sped forward until the gauge read empty.
Condemn that, mother, father. I learned denial from you.

An Argument to Walk Out On

A cup that cracked
after moderate use
shows the tracery

of its dying line,
interior stained
from what steeped

for too long
as attention strayed.
How much more

can it take, another boiling
shock poured into
its body, the waiting, the neglectful

clash into a hard sink?
There's something
to be tossed away.

It's this cup's turn
to be trash
now, before it shatters.

Kitchen

My mother so angry I would stop at the doorway
to listen for clatter, papers or silverware, edges
shaken together, or stacked in a haste
of furious attention. I'd hold my breath
and guess what the noise was about
this time and how I would go in. I'd want something
to eat, afternoons or at dusk, so I'd slide
one foot across the lit floor, slip the other in,
holding the cupboard corner. When I came to take,
there she was at the table, as if my cares
could not stack up against her endless work.
My mother's head twisted toward me, her back
bent, in a homemade jacket, her hands—
I hated that she was always busy, it tired me
to think this was life, cleaning, jotting, sewing,
reaching to slap. She read my scorn
when she glanced at me. I wanted to eat
what she worked to get, foods that might overflow
the empty pots of family. I thought,
if I pretended not to see, I would not
come into such misery, that some thin cookie
would satisfy me for an hour, like a real thing.

Cloning

When I look out the window, they are there:
father and mother, having stood for years in the weather

I left them to. I said they left me.

What makes words into yarn, spun like a snare
as invisible fingers twist them into a skein, a skin?

Scientists cloned a black-footed ferret from flesh

dead for thirty years. The baby knit anew out of stupor
kicked awake and suckled false milk. Sleek-furred,

black-eyed, aware, but without an adult

to warm against. Here, young one, I want to say,
wrap yourself in this swath, survive the seasons.

I worked it myself but never gave it to anyone.

What Did You Love About Sisley?

for my father

Was it the torn daylight stringing
winter oaks, with their empty branches,
that spoke for you, whom you thought no one heard?
You liked the snowy paintings best,

in which a single trail of footprints wandered
through the drifted lanes of French villages.
Sometimes a garden wall prickly with vines
framed human figures, minuscule in the landscape.

Fog and mist, the frozen fields, a haze
of sun over a river. As the artist did, a viewer falls
in love, forgets, for a few minutes, to fear, forgets
the loneliness, the hard stones underfoot.

Blue Jacket

After the memorial, it waited in the closet,
hung slump-shouldered while we disagreed.
Like my father, it seemed patient as we debated
who might use the caps rimmed with sweat
and Brylcreem, who'd take the worn walking stick.
The whole closet was destined for plastic bags
and the resale shop. *Someone will want these*
was our refrain. Someone who would understand
that saving—clothing and shoes and tools
and money—was the strongest lesson of life.

I lifted the blue jacket from its hook,
caught a whiff of desert dust, a reminiscence
of palo verde, always sweet after rain.
No, it did not fit me; it closed across me
with room to spare, its sleeves stretched
past my reach. The jacket was clean
and I set it down next to its kin.
Lifting the bags into the car, I was surprised
by their heft, ponderous and mum.

Since then, in dream, I wander that resale shop
as if I might see the sleeve, its color
exact in memory, the elbow cocked to rest his hands
in the pockets during evening walks. As if
I could buy back that jacket and all
that went with it: long Arizona sunsets
deepening, the quail cooing, calling out
enormous stars, the hush of footfalls
as he walked alone, but for yelps of coyotes
in the distance, their cries a ritual of family
preparing for the night.

4.

A Lover's Quarrel

A wish:
to be alive in poetry—

yet water could not teach me to write
despite the patient way it braided and unbraided
its own hair to show me

and storm did not teach me to write
despite the tree limbs it hurled over the earth
and the way it stopped to listen to the aftermath
of a particular word
before starting again with its yammer

and no, not morning glories twining
through maiden grass, wearing pale bells
that rang heedless of me

when I walked in desert, the sand did not teach me to write

when I pared a stinking
rind of cheese, to try something that had grown
old in its way
and touched it to my tongue,
that did not

What rough things could teach me to write?

a pickling vat—
the disassembling hunk of plywood
leaning against a porch not my own—
a pair of sheep clippers abandoned
frowzy with filaments

no bag of wool in sight

Night Chorus

Rural Tennessee. I lie awake
in the small motel of a small town,
the night throbbing with trills
so robust it seems impossible
that they burst from the delicate
woodwinds of frogs and crickets.
Here is a night of more than owls,
night of bobcats and weasels,
hunters in the shadows whose purpose—
to find and eat silently—slides past
the shrilling of little creatures
secreted among leaves and bark,
procreation their recreation
in early summer. Humid air
amplifies the singers' needs
and singular voices in one
hot blanket of noise, under which
the tread of a predator's foot
cannot be heard. Alone, I listen
to the power: lives driven
to wend through underworlds
on the hunt for death and sex—one
that will always come, one that may—
in a world making no distinction
whether one skulks or shouts,
feeds, fornicates, or fails
to find anything more like meaning.

Annie at 70, Hanging Wash

Does the universe have a beginning or an end? People say not,
but I can't imagine that, since every week has its Monday
of piled-up things ready to go into water, and the day
trudges through itself, filling, swirling, and lifting.
It just gets harder as time wallows past. The water shivers
from the pump, sometimes brown-tinged, but that's just dirt,
things get old. These days I drag the basket across the yard.
Dusty wind or not, have to hang things outdoors.
I like how the clothespins resemble finches perched
along the line, hooking towels and sheets in their claws.
What holds us here? Think of clouds: they don't change much,
year to year. Under the clothesline I can look up at the puffs
passing, fast or slow, doing their cloud work, or just resting,

with all the time in the world in their laps. Now that L.P.
and the boy are gone, there's less to do. I could sit,
but I don't have Missus Meyers next door anymore. She'd
be glad to know I'm the one found her, in her blue farm dress
and apron, the pretty one with flowers, in the chicken yard
but on some grass. She'd smile to hear me this way. Afternoon
coffee, by myself now, I watch the clothes flap in a little wind
as if they were walking over to visit, had a story to tell.
None of my folks went hard. That's what I'd like, a quiet inside
folding like a fist gently. I prefer to think of it that way.
Nobody knows their time before it comes. Well, the dog
knew the chickens would die by the axe, one by one, but he didn't
figure on Artie's truck with a trailer swinging loose behind it that day
along the road. Artie was sorry, of course, and I said I understood.

Cascadian Nocturne

Past midnight: an invisible world I step into
half-dressed. On a deck, a humid summer breeze
strokes my arm. The deodar cedar next door
and my Douglas-firs swing in the wind, exhale.
How much air fills one back yard.

When sounds begin in the deodar—squeaks
as of a small wheel rubbing, then low snorts,
bubbly, grunting, two, three, like contented swine
amid cedar boughs—I hold my breath.

For long minutes I listen to private lives:
the tree holding its unseen passengers, the animals—
I think, a sow raccoon and her young—
who do not expect me to be eavesdropping
in the dark, adrift in evergreen scents,

astonished by the apprisals of the night.

Nothing That Does Not Weigh

A bee killed by a spider is tied in filament
so thin only light can see it.
One leaf after another gathers rain,

collapses onto a finch's nest.
What I carry secretly—
fragments of ash, thread from a jacket seam.

One life dies and another sees.

A heart holds nothing
if it does not weigh the spider,
the awl in the heart.

What Finally Falls

These rhododendron leaves yellow
talismans of neglect. I asked you

to take on the yard, keep it
somehow. Summer

cracked our skins, though
there was little sun. Warblers

and tanagers came late, goldfinches
argued their wings. One slant

of afternoon sliced your chair. The yew's
red tears already coming out.

Where, Once

In three a.m. darkness I slide out
onto the deck. Radiant neurons shift

like stars between branches.
There's a black path

where a white owl flew.
I returned because it's real

even though gone. It's real

enough to startle spirits of wood rats
and voles crouched in the duff.

Prickle of rough planks underfoot.
A sliver may stab my flesh

if I'm careless. There's nothing I want
more than a chance. Those silent
occult wings.

Across the Country, You Are Sleeping

where bands of light
cross a windowsill,
you under a thin sheet

turn over, one limb at a time.

Lights not blue but the orange
of burnt vapor streetlights

dust along curtains and floor

and crevices of your pillow,
the grain of the bedspread

ribbed against your thumb

in a cold town
ruffled by late traffic,

your body rhythms timed
to the sounds of vehicles
gearing through the distance.

Five A.M. Finish

Wooden furniture begins
        its bronze glow, chair limbs defined

at dawn. This room, with polished
        floor, rugs a maze of patterns,

surfaces through the gloom
        slowly, like our talk

which hesitates along angles
        and curves that rise

from shadows, after the night.
        A soft peep from your watch

tells the hour, as if time's pasture
        held nestlings.

We sit with hands quiet
        on chair arms. We wait

as silence fills with purple that turns
        to rose, then gold,

as a junco outside
        the window notices our shapes,

strange at the early hour, in this
        artificial hollow that the bird

can see but cannot fly into:
        a shell, something about us

from which—we don't know
        why—we can't emerge.

Photograph, French Village

Side by side, two old men
in brown jackets, their berets
atilt as they lounge in the plaza

of this hamlet, on benches
where retired friends sit out the heat

of afternoon while they discuss today's
game of *pétanque*. Near us, metal clinks
as the orbs nudge each other familiarly.

I'm a visitor, twenty, in love with France.
I can't help saying so, and the men beam,

so I ask to photograph them, and they agree
for this nice young lady, far from her home.
How many travelers have such luck? When,

months later, I send a copy of the photo
to the address one of them scrawled on a map,
I receive back a postcard with *Embrasse, embrasse*
over an unreadable signature.

And who by chance might meet a stranger
with a camera who will take your picture
with your best friend, on your favorite bench,

listening to the soft talk of metal boules
kissing each other's silver cheeks?

The Loire in Flood

In the muscles of a river, I rediscovered my love.
Hummocks of water shivered in a standing wave.

It must have been strong but I had no fear.

Think how flood reaches each watcher onshore:
the rumor of rising, disbelief that shudders
each pebble and tussock as they start to go under,

and, in the hedgerow, startlement
of a bird's strange word: a corn crake, hidden,
watching what it knew transformed.

You swayed beside me, seized by the shadows of trees.

Tap

Gray end of a day that seems like
a month of rain. A pub nests where
two lanes meet in an English village.
Sheep smells hang from the straw
that stuffs the roof. We push into
the peaty fug. *O yes, the child,
come in boy, it's warm.* Hearth
gives the room a scent of armpits,
humid with honest work, spilled
beer on farm boots. *O yes. There's
some roast left even this late in the
day, there's rarebit.* Fragments
of cheddar on our plates. The woman
lets the boy run among trestle tables,
with only the other two gentlemen
at the bar, who smile over their
whiskers. *We've a bit of custom
at the odd hour. Hasn't it poured,
it's always like this in January.
You'll have another.*
So we do.

If, Then

No, the day offered no promises, given
the thin towels in a French hotel, the long
narrow bones of stairway winding around
the spine of an elevator that did not operate,
given the tilt of floors the color of dried blood,
unwelcoming dimness that had shadowed
a hundred years of guests used to walking up
with string bags of cheeses, baguettes,
and bottles of wine clanging like hearts
on a wedding day—one might not hope,
on the fifth-floor landing, for a small table
topped with lace and a vase with one violet
whose petals pointed toward a door
with a number matching the key
that rattled like a shackle in the keyhole, one
might not have thought there was any promise
of apricot sun sweetening the slate rooftops
beyond open shutters, with even the flying bugs
winging in and out in a freedom that felt like love.

ACKNOWLEDGMENTS

Thanks to the editors of the following publications in which some of these poems, or versions thereof, previously appeared:

After Hours: "Annie at 70, Hanging Wash" (Mary Blinn Poetry Prize finalist 2021); "Blue Jacket" (Mary Blinn Poetry Prize finalist 2022)

Bacopa Literary Review: "The Point that Divides the Sea"

Black Horse Review: "What's Going to Kill You"

Bloodroot: "Instar"

Catamaran: "Orcas, A Prelude"

Caustic Frolic: "What Finally Falls"

Cirque: "Kitchen"

Connecticut Poetry Society: "Infection: Tether and Needle" (Connecticut Poetry Prize honorable mention 2022)

Cutthroat: "Ritual for Beasts"

Dodging the Rain: "October Salmon"

Feral: A Journal of Poetry and Art: "Fire-Nerves"

Frontier Poetry: "Listening for Otters" (Nature and Place Contest finalist)

In Parentheses: "An Argument to Walk Out On"; "Duende Verde"

Little Patuxent Review: "Not Interested in Jesus"

Live Encounters: Poetry and Writing: "Cascadian Nocturne"; "Solo Dance"

Quartet: "Cloning"

PacificREVIEW: "Across the Country, You Are Sleeping"

Rattle: Poets Respond: "The Boy in the Well"

River and South Review: "Wolf Moon"

Salamander: "Night Chorus"

Sheila-Na-Gig: "Understory"

Speckled Trout Review: "35-Cent Gas"

Spillway: "Unable Now to Atone"

Terrain: "If One Can Speak Seriously of the Sublime"

Texas Poetry Calendar 2022: "Desert Devotions"

Third Wednesday: "Torrential" (Special Merit, Annual Poetry Contest 2021)

West Trade Review: "Nourished"

Why Horses? Red Mare #13: "Last Crocus"

Willawaw Journal: "If, Then"; "Photograph, French Village"

Writers Rising Up: "What Did You Love About Sisley?" (Bill Holm Witness Poetry Award 2023)

* * *

Many thanks to my cherished writer friends, including workshop leaders whose kind attention helped me develop some of the poems in this collection: Ellen Bass, Keetje Kuipers, Melissa Kwasny, Paul Nelson, Carl Phillips, David Wagoner, and especially Gary Copeland Lilley. I am also grateful to my workshop colleagues, whose affection and insights have sustained me over the rigors of recent years: Kelli Russell Agodon, Tom Aslin, Susan Bates, Kris Becker, Anne Bergeron, Ronda Piszk Broatch, Sharon Carter, Lauren Davis, Risa Denenberg, Pam Dionne, Joanne Durham, Deb Hammond, M. Michael Hanner, Toni Hanner, Susan Harter, Gayle Kaune, Susan Landgraf, Susanna Lang, Jenifer Browne

Lawrence, Lisa Low, Niamh MacConchradha (Nelly Crowe), Ellie Mathews, Tom Mitchell, Kathy O'Fallon, Bethany Reid, Dora Robinson, Karen Seashore, Carla Shafer, Jess Skyleson, Juanita Smart, Sarah Dickenson Snyder, Diana Taylor, Lauren Tess, David Thornbrugh, Francine Walls, Diane Hueter Warner, Richard Widerkehr, Kris Wolverton, Sarah Young, and Carl Youngmann.

At Cornerstone Press, thanks to Dr. Ross K. Tangedal and staffers Eva Nielsen, Gabby Sullivan, Allison Lange, Sophie McPherson, Ava Willett, Madison Schultz, and Autumn Vine.

Sharing our creative work is a gift to the world as well as to each other.

Jayne Marek earned a Ph.D. from the University of Wisconsin–Madison and an M.F.A. from the University of Notre Dame. Nominated for Best of the Net and Pushcart Prizes, she won the Last Stanza Poetry Journal Editor's Choice Award and the Bill Holm Witness Poetry Prize. She held residencies at Playa, the Whiteley Center, and Hypatia-in-the-Woods. Her writings and photographs appeared in dozens of publications, including *Rattle, Terrain, Catamaran, Calyx, The New York Times, Spillway, Bloodroot, Salamander, Northwest Review, Cutthroat, Gulf Stream*, and elsewhere, and she provided cover photos for *Typehouse, Chestnut Review, Silk Road, Bombay Gin, Amsterdam Quarterly's 2018 Yearbook*, and *The Bend*, as well as for four poetry books.

Prior full-length poetry collections included *Dusk-Voiced* (2024), *The Tree Surgeon Dreams of Bowling* (2018), and *In and Out of Rough Water* (2017). Her scholarly work included *Women Editing Modernism: "Little" Magazines and Literary History* (1995) and the *Index to Poetry Magazine* covering the years 1912–1997 (Modern Poetry Association 1998). She received two fellowships from the National Endowment for the Humanities for literary scholarship. She made her home in the Pacific Northwest, near the wild and beautiful coast, prior to passing away in January 2025.

www.ingramcontent.com/pod-product-compliance
Lightning Source LLC
Chambersburg PA
CBHW030504130626
46549CB00007B/2850